This book is to be returned on or before
the last date stamped below.

1 1 JUL 2001

2 6 SEP 2006

NEW PERSPECTIVES
The War in Former Yugoslavia

NATHANIEL HARRIS

WAYLAND

First published in 1997 by
Wayland Publishers Ltd,
61 Western Road,
Hove,
East Sussex BN3 1JD

This book was prepared for Wayland Publishers Ltd
by Ruth Nason.

Series editor: Alex Woolf
Series design: Stonecastle Graphics
Book design: LNbooks, Houghton Regis, Bedfordshire

Find Wayland on the internet at:
http://www.wayland.co.uk

British Library Cataloguing in Publication Data
Harris, Nathaniel, 1937-
  The war in former Yugoslavia. - (New perspectives)
  1. Yugoslav War, 1991- - Juvenile literature
  I. Title
  949.7'1'03

ISBN 0 7502 2053 8

Printed and bound in Italy by G. Canale & C.S.p.A., Turin

Cover photos: A Serb
soldier; Dubrovnik on fire
after Serb shelling.

Page 1: Terrified families
leave Dubrovnik on a
coastal steamer, as
shells rain down on
the besieged city.

Acknowledgements

The Author and Publishers thank the following for their permission
to reproduce photographs: Camera Press: cover (left) and pages 10b,
12b, 23, 28, 29b, 36, 39, 40, 42, 44, 46, 47, 48, 50, 51, 59; Hulton-Getty
Picture Collection: pages 7 (Kevin Weaver), 12t, 13, 16, 31 (Kevin
Weaver), 34b (Kevin Weaver); Popperfoto: page 17; Popperfoto/AFP:
cover (right) and pages 1, 5, 6, 19, 25, 30; Popperfoto/EPA: pages 26,
34t; Popperfoto/Reuters: pages 32, 45, 52, 56; Topham Picturepoint:
pages 3, 4, 10t, 11, 14, 15, 18, 20, 21, 22, 24, 27, 29, 37, 38, 41, 43, 53,
54, 55.

CONTENTS

Croat soldiers burn the Yugoslav flag.

SARAJEVO, A CHANGED CITY

As it was: Sarajevo, the capital city of Bosnia. Until the early 1990s, Bosnia was one of six republics that made up Yugoslavia.

Sarajevo, the capital of Bosnia, on 5 April 1992. The peace march began with a few people who gathered in the west of the city. As they headed for the city centre, more and more came to join them. Eventually there were about 7,000 marchers, belonging to most of the main groups in Yugoslavia. Among them were Muslims, Serbs and Croats, as well as people who thought of themselves as simply Yugoslavs. Many of the marchers were young people, and they were waving Yugoslav flags.

They were on the move because there had been trouble in their country, and it was threatening to get worse. It looked as though Yugoslavia was breaking up, and its different peoples were becoming more and more angry with one another. Serious fighting

Marching for peace

'We were there because we thought there was still time to change people's minds, to save Sarajevo ... as a place where Muslims, Serbs and Croats could live together as they had for five hundred years ... The idea was to ... show that the city still belonged to the people – all the people.'

(Samir Koric, a young accountant who took part in the peace march.)

A politician's view

Politicians were less certain about their safety in Sarajevo than the unarmed peace marchers. The Bosnian Serb leader Radovan Karadzic claimed to feel threatened in his hotel room. He described the night of 4 April 1992:

'The atmosphere in Sarajevo was that of terror. The streets were deserted and, from our offices in the Holiday Inn, we could see Muslim Green Beret snipers placed on top of high buildings. Everything was blocked and we could not leave the hotel.'

involving Serbs and Croats had already broken out in the north of the country. Now Bosnia was threatening to leave Yugoslavia, to the anger of the Bosnian Serbs. In Sarajevo itself, some Serbs and Muslims were already exchanging shots.

The marchers wanted to show that people of all kinds could stand together against division, hatred and bloodshed. At the same time, few of them believed that there would be a full-scale war in Bosnia or, if there was, that people who lived in Sarajevo would get deeply involved. After all, their city was a large, lively, modern-minded place whose citizens were easy-going and mixed freely. So the mood on the march was cheerful, matching the sunny weather.

The day after the peace march: a Bosnian government soldier and a group of civilians under fire from Serb snipers.

June 1992: the upper storeys of the tallest building in Sarajevo are burned out after a night of heavy shelling.

When they reached the city centre, the leaders of the march stopped at the parliament building to hold talks. The rest of the crowd moved on, determined to win as much support as possible. Unaware that fighting had already started in the southern area of Sarajevo, they marched on steadily in that direction. Shots rang out and a man was wounded, but at first nobody understood what was happening. Then there were more shots, and the crowd broke and ran.

One girl did not run. Suada Dilberovic, a medical student, had fallen to the ground with a bullet lodged in her chest. She was rushed to hospital, but she was dead before she got there. Most of the scattered marchers did not even know that Sarajevo had suffered its first civilian casualty.

Nor did the leaders, who were making passionate speeches in the square in front of the parliament building. But within a few hours they were also being fired on. Each side blamed the other, while the fighting grew more intense. Soon no one could doubt that a war had started.

Sarajevans humbled

For some people, the former prosperity of Sarajevo made conditions even harder to bear. A woman who had formerly been a judge said sadly:

'When you see me now, it is not as I really am. I am not this dirty, poor woman, in dirty smelly clothes, that all my perfume cannot cover.'

Ashamed of borrowing and accepting gifts from foreign friends, she told the American writer David Rieff:

'You see, we are beggars ... The war has corrupted all of us. I'm not sure we will ever recover. The buildings can be rebuilt ... But we have become damaged goods – a generation of shell-shocked beggars.'

After the war

The war lasted for almost four years. A long, cruel siege left Sarajevo completely changed. Its citizens were frightened and shabby, its big modern buildings in ruins, and the streets pockmarked with bullet holes and shrapnel scars.

Many of the people had changed, too. Peace had returned at last, but wartime feelings of hatred and fear had not gone away. Under the peace agreement, Sarajevo would be run by a council with a Muslim majority. But thousands of Serbs refused to live under the control of people they now thought of as enemies. They packed up and left the city, making for areas where their fellow-Serbs were in charge. They were so angry that they could not bear the idea of enemies taking over their old homes. Before leaving, they set fire to their houses. When firemen arrived, they were driven off with grenades. New, burned-out ruins added to the destruction of war.

Some people had kept alive their memories of the old Sarajevo. They tried not to hate their neighbours because they were 'different'. But friendship and trust would clearly take a long time to repair – longer, perhaps, than the broken buildings.

For months, Sarajevans had no gas or electricity supplies. This couple are taking their sofa to a market, to sell as firewood.

THE MAKING OF YUGOSLAVIA

The peoples of Yugoslavia

Until very recently Yugoslavia was the largest state in south-eastern Europe, the region known as the Balkans. It was also the home of many peoples, including Slovenes, Croats, Serbs, Montenegrins, Albanians and Macedonians.

Yugoslavia existed for just over seventy years, from 1918 to 1991. However, the peoples of Yugoslavia had lived there for much longer. Despite their different names, most of them were descended from one group of tribes, the South Slavs, who moved into the Balkans from the fifth century AD. The main exception, the Albanians, were non-Slavs who had established themselves in the region even earlier.

Over the next few hundred years, the South Slavs broke up into separate peoples. Those in the west, the Slovenes and Croats, were converted to the Roman Catholic form of Christianity that dominated western Europe. Their culture was based on Latin, they used the Roman alphabet, and they were 'western' in many other respects. The Serbs, Montenegrins and Macedonians also became Christians, but they followed the Orthodox Church, used a Greek-based alphabet, and developed their own distinct culture. The west-east separation was remarkably complete; for example, even though the Croatian and Serbian languages remained almost identical, Croats and Serbs came to feel that they were utterly different from each other.

Yugoslavia's position in Europe, 1945-92.

Yugoslavia in 1991. This map shows former Yugoslavia just before it broke up: a land of many peoples, often living side by side in mixed communities.

In 1900 Eastern Europe was still dominated by the empires of Austria-Hungary, Russia and Ottoman Turkey. The decline of Turkey, and the collapse of Austria-Hungary in 1918, made possible the creation of Yugoslavia.

Later events sharpened such differences. The Slovenes, and later the Croats, became subjects of the Habsburg Austrian empire. This empire became a Christian outpost in a long struggle against the Turks, who overran most of the Balkans. Among the Turks' victims were the Serbs, who went down fighting at Kosovo in 1389.

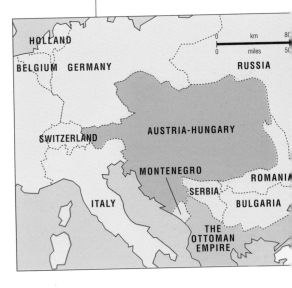

The Turks controlled most of the Balkans from the fourteenth to the nineteenth century. They were Muslims, ruling mainly Christian peoples. But in some places a substantial number of their subjects became converts to Islam, the religion of Muslims. When the Turks were driven out of the region, these converts remained faithful to Islam. Most of them were Albanians, Croats or Serbs, like their neighbours, but because of their religion they came to be seen as a separate people. Their enemies often labelled them 'Turks', to make them seem more foreign.

The Turkish bridge at Mostar (above) was a tourist attraction.
In 1994 it was destroyed (below) when Serb forces besieged the town.

So by 1900 the main ethnic groups had formed in what later became Yugoslavia. 'Ethnic' is a useful term, used to describe peoples or national communities, whether their identity is based on skin colour, language, religion, or less clear-cut ideas such as a shared way of life. Ethnic conflicts involve groups or peoples who think of one another as deeply and hatefully different. Beliefs of this kind, based on prejudice, often lead to savage persecutions and wars.

The First World War

By the 1900s the Turks were in retreat and the Austro-Hungarian empire was expanding into the Balkans. The Serbs had won their independence from Turkey in 1878. Now they wanted to free their fellow Serbs in the large province of Bosnia-Herzegovina (usually shortened to 'Bosnia'),

which was occupied by the Austrians. On 28 June 1914 Serb revolutionaries murdered the heir to the Austrian throne, Franz Ferdinand, while he was visiting the Bosnian capital, Sarajevo. The Austrians replied by launching an invasion of Serbia. Then other great European powers became involved in the conflict, and by 4 August 1914 the First World War had broken out.

During the First World War, Serbia was overrun by Austrian and Bulgarian forces. Here, Serb refugees are leaving Macedonia, under the protection of an Orthodox monk.

The creation of Yugoslavia

The war cost millions of lives and led to the collapse of several great European empires. One of these was Austria-Hungary – which meant that the former Austrian provinces of Slovenia, Croatia and Bosnia could decide their own futures. In December 1918 the main South Slav peoples agreed to set up a new state with the king of Serbia as its head. At first it was known as the Kingdom of the Serbs, Croats and Slovenes, but its name was changed in 1929 to Yugoslavia, 'land of the South Slavs'.

Early enthusiasm for unity soon weakened. Non-Serbs felt that they had too little say in the running of the

King Alexander I of Yugoslavia (left) at the christening of his son, Peter, 1923. On the right are the Duke and Duchess of York, later King George VI and Queen Elizabeth of Great Britain.

kingdom, and the Croats became particularly discontented. For long periods no parliament met and the king ruled as a dictator. There continued to be trouble, and in 1934 Croatian conspirators assassinated King Alexander I while he was on a visit to France.

The Second World War

The situation was still uncertain when the Second World War broke out in 1939. This war was caused by the aggressions of Nazi Germany, led by Adolf Hitler. One country after another fell to the Germans, and in 1941 it was Yugoslavia's turn.

The German victory was swift and Yugoslavia was divided between Germany and two of its allies, fascist Italy and Hungary. The Germans also set up Croat and Serb states, run by people they could trust. In Croatia, the Ustasha movement led by Ante Pavelic was given power.

The Second World War: the boys in this camp have been forced to become Catholics and wear uniforms carrying the insignia of the Croatian Ustasha movement. Their parents have probably already been murdered.

The Ustasha terror

Ustasha atrocities shocked even their allies. A report by the German SS, the black-uniformed security troops, notorious for mass murders, reads:

'The Ustasha units have carried out atrocities not only against male Orthodox of military age, but in particular in the most bestial fashion against men, women and children.'

The Ustasha view was expressed by one of the leaders, Victor Gutic, in May 1941:

'Every Croat who takes the side of the Serbs is not only not a good Croat but an opponent of our plan for cleansing our Croatia of unwanted elements. Let us call on the mercy of God if that patriotic labour sometimes oversteps the usual bounds of religious morals and ethics.'

The Ustasha shared Nazi ideas about destroying 'inferior' peoples: they turned on the large Serb minority in Croatia, murdering hundreds of thousands and forcing others to convert to Catholicism. Like the Nazis, the Ustasha also murdered Jews and gypsies.

Many Yugoslavs continued to resist the Germans and their allies. Because the Germans were so much stronger, the Yugoslavs rarely fought pitched battles against them. Instead they used ambushes and sabotage to weaken the enemy, hiding out in the mountains when the Germans attacked in force. This kind of fighting is called guerrilla warfare.

The Germans tried to bomb the strongholds of the Yugoslav guerrillas in Bosnia.

The Yugoslav resistance was divided into two groups who fought each other as well as the Germans. The Chetniks were almost all Serbs, determined to bring back the king, Peter II, once the war was over. Their rivals, the Partisans, had some support from all ethnic groups and were ably led by an experienced revolutionary, Josip Broz, better known as Tito, a name he used in his secret work. As the war turned against Germany and the German army retreated, the Partisans took over. The Chetniks were destroyed and Tito became the leader of post-war Yugoslavia.

A Second World War scene. Mounted Partisans, members of Yugoslavia's anti-Nazi resistance, talk with a British soldier. British officers and men were dropped into Yugoslavia by parachute to help the Partisans.

Yugoslavia as a Communist state

Tito and his followers were Communists, and they rapidly turned Yugoslavia into a Communist state. In theory, Communism meant that ordinary working people took over political power and controlled the factories, farms and other forms of wealth. In practice, everything was run by the Communist Party. No other political parties were allowed, and every other form of opposition was also suppressed.

Yugoslavia also joined the large East European group of Communist states led by the Soviet Union (present-

Yugoslavism

Tito's slogan as leader of Yugoslavia was 'Brotherhood and Unity', but in the early 1970s he had to crack down on a strong nationalist movement in Croatia. In a moment of frankness he told an interviewer:

'Yugoslavism? It does not exist, but maybe one day in the future it will come.'

Sarajevo, 1980

Richard West, a British expert on Yugoslav affairs, noted how important Tito had become to Yugoslavs. In his book *Tito and the Rise and Fall of Yugoslavia* West writes:

'In February 1980 Sarajevo struck me as cheerful and confident ... The only cloud on the future was Tito's illness and approaching death. "If Tito goes, do you think we'll all start killing each other again?" I heard a man asking his friends in a café.'

Holiday-makers in Lapad, Yugoslavia, one of many sunny coastal resorts that were very popular until fighting started in the early 1990s. The damage done to the tourist trade made recovery from the war even more difficult.

day Russia and several of its neighbours). This bloc was opposed by the North Atlantic Treaty Organization (NATO), an anti-Communist alliance led by the USA.

Then, in 1948, Tito quarrelled with the Soviet dictator, Stalin, and left the Communist alliance. By standing up for Yugoslavia, Tito increased his popularity at home. And although Yugoslavia remained a Communist state, the USA and its allies were eager to support any enemy of the Soviet Union. As a result, Yugoslavia's economy boomed, helped by the development of a major tourist industry. For several decades, Tito's Yugoslavia seemed to be a success.

THINGS FALL APART

President Tito in London, 1978.

Life under Tito

In reality, Yugoslavia under Tito was never as prosperous as outsiders believed. To keep the people happy, workers were well paid and high-quality goods were brought in from abroad. But many of the goods were bought with loans, and Yugoslavia's debts mounted steadily. By the 1970s, debt, rising prices and unemployment were creating serious problems. The future began to look uncertain.

This is the kind of situation in which ethnic hatreds can flare up in a formerly peaceful community. When times are hard, people become anxious and look for someone to blame – and the easiest targets are groups who are

Contrasting memories

Looking back on the Tito era in the 1990s, a hotel receptionist told the author Richard West:

'You hear people say how awful it was under the Communists. It was wonderful under the Communists! The hotels were full. Everyone could travel the country or go abroad. People of different religions were friendly with each other.'

On the other hand, a cynical Croat told BBC reporter Martin Bell:

'Yes, we lived in peace and harmony. We lived in peace and harmony because every hundred metres we had a policeman to make sure we loved one another very much.'

seen as 'different'. Instead of pulling together, people think of one another as rivals.

This was true of neighbours, and also of different parts of Yugoslavia. An important source of trouble was the fact that Slovenia and Croatia were more industrialized and better-off than the rest of the country. Slovenes and Croats felt that too much of their wealth was used to raise the living standards of other Yugoslavs. On their side, these others envied the Slovenes and Croats, and felt that these two republics ought to do more for their fellow-Yugoslavs! By the start of the 1970s the Croats were demanding self-government or even independence. But Tito was still firmly in control and their movement was suppressed – for the time being.

Sarajevo in happier times, as the host of the 1984 Winter Olympics. The photograph was taken at the opening ceremony in the Olympic stadium, now a cemetery.

How Yugoslavia was governed

Tito had always recognized the importance of ethnic differences, and this affected the way that Communist Yugoslavia was organized. It was a federation – a league of republics, each with a good deal of control over its local affairs. Issues that affected Yugoslavia as a whole were decided by a central (federal) Yugoslav government in Belgrade. For example, foreign policy was decided by the federal government, and the Yugoslav army was a federal force, drawn from all ethnic groups. The six republics (Slovenia, Croatia, Bosnia, Montenegro, Serbia, Macedonia) and two provinces (Kosovo and Vojvodina) had their own governments and parliaments. Like the federal government, they were all under Communist control.

The federal arrangement of Yugoslavia did not mean that the peoples of the country were neatly separated, each living in its own republic. In most of the republics the populations were mixed. In Croatia, for example, the majority were Croats, but there were also very many Serbs, as well as smaller numbers belonging to other groups. A similar situation existed elsewhere. In one republic, Bosnia, there was no single group forming a majority, since the inhabitants included three large communities, Muslims, Serbs and Croats.

If all of Yugoslavia's peoples could live together in peace, this mixing of populations would not matter. But if old hatreds came back to life and Yugoslavia started to break up, the situation in the individual republics might easily become serious.

Women weep at the funeral of President Tito in 1980.

New leaders

Tito's power and prestige remained intact right down to his death in 1980. The presidency of Yugoslavia then passed to a group of Communist leaders, one representing each of the republics and provinces. Each member of this group presidency had a turn at being its chairman for a year.

These new leaders found it much harder to hold the system together, although they tried to share power fairly between the republics. As the economy continued to weaken, many citizens lost faith in the government and the Communist system.

Politicians of a new kind began to come forward, speaking for a single nation or ethnic group. One leader of this sort was Franjo Tudjman, a Croat who had fought as a Partisan in the Second World War and had for a time been a Communist. As early as the 1960s he had become a Croat nationalist, and a period spent in prison made him a hero in the eyes of his fellow-Croats. As the Communist grip on Yugoslavia weakened during the 1980s, Tudjman waited for his chance.

Franjo Tudjman, 1996. Behind him is the Croatian coat of arms.

> ## Tudjman of Croatia
>
> Franjo Tudjman (1922-) became leader of the Croatian Democratic Union in 1989. In 1990, when the Communists allowed other parties to take part in elections, he was elected president of Croatia.
>
> The Serbs in Croatia were afraid of what would happen to them if Croatia became independent with Tudjman in control. In his writings, Tudjman had argued that Second World War crimes against Jews and Serbs had been exaggerated. His admirers in the 1990s claimed that he had changed, but he could still make remarks such as 'Thank God my wife is not a Jew or a Serb', and put forward the claim that Bosnia should be part of Croatia.

In Serbia, a new leader emerged in 1987 after a struggle inside the Communist Party. Communism was supposed to unite all peoples, but the struggle was won by an aggressive Serb nationalist, Slobodan Milosevic. The Serbs were the largest ethnic group in Yugoslavia (36 per cent of the population), and they had staunch allies in the Montenegrins. To judge by his

Slobodan Milosevic
speaking in Belgrade in
1989.

actions, Milosevic intended to make the Serbs dominant within the Yugoslav federation, or else to create an independent 'Greater Serbia' by adding all the Serb-occupied lands in Croatia and Bosnia to the existing Serb republic.

Milosevic's ruthlessness was shown by the campaigns he launched in 1987 against Yugoslavia's two provinces, Kosovo and Vojvodina. The provinces were not full republics. They were linked with Serbia, but their populations included very large numbers of non-Serbs. For this reason, they had been allowed to run their own affairs.

In Vojvodina there was only a small Serb majority, and in Kosovo Serbs were actually in a minority. Kosovo was a famous name in Serb history (because of the great battle against the Turks in 1389), but times had changed. By the 1980s the population was over-whelmingly Albanian. Only 10 per cent were Serbs, and Milosevic claimed that the Albanians were persecuting them and trying to drive them out. There had certainly been trouble in Kosovo, but the main reason was probably its poverty. People in Kosovo were actually worse off than people anywhere else in Yugoslavia. Nevertheless Milosevic declared that Kosovo and Vojvodina ought to be brought back under

Milosevic of Serbia

Slobodan Milosevic (1941-) became the head of the Serbian League of Communists and, from 1989, president of Serbia.

At mass meetings, he made passionate speeches, promising to defend fellow-Serbs in Kosovo and elsewhere. However, many political experts thought that his policies were shrewd rather than sincere. BBC correspondent Mischa Glenny questioned

'whether Slobodan Milosevic himself was really a nationalist or simply a ... ruthless politician who came to believe ... that in order to hold on to power he had to play on Serb nationalist feeling.'

Kosovo and the Serbs

To the Serbs, Kosovo was a holy place. They still remembered the battle there, in 1389, against the Turks. To Serbs, this made it their land forever. A modern Serb writer, Matija Beckovic, declared that:

'Kosovo would be Serbian even if there were not a single Serb living there.'

The head of a Serbian convent in Kosovo, allegedly attacked by Albanians.

direct Serb rule, and when he said this at mass meetings in Serbia, huge crowds cheered him on.

Milosevic's threats and political manoeuvring succeeded in ousting the local leaders and replacing them with his own followers. By 1989 the two provinces had rejoined Serbia, though not without Albanian resistance and much violence.

Serbs and Albanians

Serb nationalism was gaining strength in the 1980s, even before Milosevic started to champion it. In 1986 a petition to the Serbian government was signed by two hundred Serb intellectuals – writers and scholars who wanted something done about 'the unbearable condition of the Serb nation in Kosovo'. They claimed that the Albanian majority was committing genocide – 'race murder' – against the Serbs in the province:

'Old women and nuns are raped, frail children beaten up ... churches and historic holy places desecrated ... people forced to sell their property for nothing.'

Albanians dismissed these charges as wild exaggerations. After Milosevic had taken over the province, the writer Shkelzen Maliqi declared that:

'The Serbs, a privileged minority, rule over Kosovo with the aid of the police and the army.'

The collapse of Communism

Milosevic's harsh treatment of the provinces made other Yugoslav republics more fearful of Serb domination. So the republics insisted more strongly on their individual rights. Their rulers, although fellow-Communists, found it increasingly difficult to work together. At the same time, great changes were taking place all over Eastern Europe, where Communist dictatorships were collapsing. The disunited Yugoslav Communists knew they could not resist change, and so they allowed other political parties to form and take part in elections.

Many of the new parties took a strong nationalist line, championing their own ethnic group or republic. During 1990, nationalists won all the elections held in the Yugoslav republics. Among the new governing parties was the Croatian Democratic Union led by Franjo Tudjman, who now took control in Croatia. The Communists were defeated everywhere except in Serbia and Montenegro, where the party (renamed the Socialist Party) had adopted Milosevic's nationalist outlook.

There were still many people who called themselves Yugoslavs rather than Slovenes, Croats or Serbs. But the elections showed that the majority had been won over to narrower loyalties. It looked as though Yugoslavia would soon fall apart.

March 1991: the Yugoslav army moves into Belgrade after an anti-government demonstration.

YUGOSLAVIA AT WAR

During the early months of 1991, talks were still being held in the hope of keeping the republics together and saving Yugoslavia. But the Serbs would not give way on any important point, and from the start the Slovenes, led by Milan Kucan, seemed determined to leave the federation. As the arguments grew more heated, the Serbs put themselves in the wrong by blocking the appointment of a Croat as chairman of the group presidency. Not surprisingly, in May 1991 a large majority of Croats voted in favour of the idea that Croatia was a sovereign state – that is, fully independent and with the power to leave Yugoslavia if it wanted to.

Serbs in Croatia demonstrate against separation from Yugoslavia.

66 Milosevic's threat

As Croatia moved towards independence, the Serbian leader, Milosevic, made his attitude clear. In March 1991 he declared:

'We do not dispute the right of the Croatian nation to secede [break away] from Yugoslavia if that nation decides of its own free will ... but ... no one should think that a part of the Serbian nation will be allowed to go with them. Because the history of the Serbian nation in the independent state of Croatia [under Ustasha rule during the Second World War] is too tragic to risk such a fate again.' 99

Croatia did not leave the federation at once, but by this time the 600,000 Serbs in the republic were thoroughly alarmed. This was partly the fault of Tudjman's government, which made them feel they were strangers who did not belong in a Croat state. Under Tudjman, many Serbs in Croatia lost their jobs, especially in government service or the police force. In some country areas where Croats were in the majority, Serbs were attacked or threatened, and elsewhere Serbs did the same to Croats. When the Croatian Serbs held a referendum that declared their opposition to the separation of Croatia from Yugoslavia, Tudjman condemned it as illegal.

26 June 1991: the parliament of Croatia proclaims the republic's independence.

War in Slovenia and Croatia

In this tense situation, Slovenia and Croatia finally decided to break away on 25 June 1991. Armed clashes in Croatia grew fiercer, but the most sensational news came from Slovenia. There, aiming to prevent the establishment of the new state, the Yugoslav army attacked the border posts set up by the Slovenes. The Slovenes fought back, and did surprisingly well, rapidly surrounding many of the Yugoslav army garrisons stationed in Slovenia.

After a ten-day war, a truce was arranged by the European Community (now the European Union), and over the next few weeks the Yugoslav army withdrew. Nobody admitted it, but this meant that Slovenia could not be stopped from leaving the federation – unless the rest of the world refused to recognize the new state.

The army's failure in Slovenia damaged the Yugoslav federation. But it was easy for the Serbs and others to accept Slovenian independence because the minority groups in the republic were small.

27 June 1991: in the capital of Slovenia, Ljubljana, people block the roads with buses and trucks to hold up the Yugoslav army.

Croatia was quite different. The Serbs of Croatia were determined to resist Tudjman's government, and they had arms of their own as well as arms smuggled in from Serbia. The Yugoslav army was soon involved. Some of its leaders wanted to hold the federation together and believed that the actions of Slovenia and Croatia were illegal. But most of the army officers were Serbs, and acted out of blind loyalty to their own people. In some places the army intervened to keep the peace, but more often it took the Serb side, giving the rebels a tremendous advantage.

The war in Croatia was a savage affair, full of senseless murders and mutilations of innocent people. Many of the worst things were not done by regular soldiers but by militias – armed groups, or gangs, of Serbs or Croats who soon became used to a wild, brutal way of life. The Croat militias included 'Ustasha' – fighters who deliberately took over the name and the symbols of the Second World War fascists who had massacred Serbs and Jews. Serb groups calling themselves Chetniks, Tigers or White Eagles were equally fanatical and ruthlessly violent.

Local warlords controlled many areas, supervising what later became known as 'ethnic cleansing'. This meant driving out – or killing – everybody in the area who did not belong to the ethnic group that was in control. While the Serbs were winning, this meant that thousands of Croats became refugees. Later, millions of Yugoslavs from other ethnic backgrounds would become homeless.

Members of one of the Serb militias, the Chetniks, practise their shooting.

The slaughter 'unstoppable'

The soldiers of the Yugoslav army in Croatia were not all Serbs. BBC correspondent Mischa Glenny met a Macedonian who had been sent, unwillingly, to the front in Croatia and later deserted. According to this man:

'Mutual slaughter occurred on both sides. In Karadzicevo, the Croats slaughtered a large group of aged Serbs, while in one incident in a village taken by the Serbs, the Chetniks threw a grenade into a bomb shelter where fifteen Croat civilians had taken refuge ... As far as I could work out, the Croats had provoked a lot of the nastiness in the first place but searching for the one who started it is a waste of time. Once it had started the massacres were unstoppable.'

Unexpected horrors

Mischa Glenny was as surprised as other experts on Eastern Europe by the savage turn of events in Yugoslavia. In his book *The Fall of Yugoslavia* he writes:

'Before May 1991, Croats and Serbs lived together in relative contentment throughout the regions which have now been so dreadfully ravaged. They were perfectly aware that the ... Yugoslav state was entering troubled seas. Yet nobody in their wildest fantasy would have predicted that within a little more than twelve months, the peaceful town of Vukovar would be levelled to the ground in one of the most merciless bombardments of modern history. Nor would they have dreamed it possible that Croat soldiers would massacre innocent Serbs, while Serb fighters would mutilate innocent Croats.'

Vukovar, devastated by the Serb-Croat war of 1991.

As well as death, the war inflicted terrible destruction. The ancient and beautiful Croatian port of Dubrovnik endured a long siege, and the town of Vukovar was pounded into rubble before it finally fell to the Serbs.

The Croats were not prepared for war, and the awkward shape of Croatia made it hard to defend; its southernmost regions, heavily inhabited by Serbs, were drawn out in two long, widely separated strips, with the Bosnian republic between them. By the autumn of 1991 the Serbs had won control of a third of Croatia. They held on to their gains, and in January 1992 the Croats were forced to accept a cease-fire. The Serbs had triumphed.

The breakup continues

Meanwhile, the breakup of Yugoslavia had continued. In September 1991, Macedonia declared itself independent. A month later the Bosnian parliament did the same. However, parliament's decision needed to be confirmed by a vote of the Bosnian people. And since the population of the republic included three very substantial ethnic groups, this might well lead to trouble.

Supporters of Croatia demonstrate at Maastricht for recognition of the republic by the EC. They hold portraits of Ante Pavelic, leader of the infamous Ustasha in Croatia during the Second World War.

The situation in Yugoslavia worried other countries, and also international organizations such as the European Community (EC) and the United Nations (UN). It was the EC that arranged the cease-fire in Slovenia and, less successfully, a series of cease-fires during the fighting in Croatia. Most countries would have liked Yugoslavia to stay as it was. They realized that, once things fall apart, chaos can spread and keep on spreading until it engulfs other states and peoples. However, the determination of the Slovenes and Croats made an impression. Germany decided to recognize the new republics, and by early 1992 other EC members felt that they might as well do the same.

A danger foreseen

Should other countries recognize Slovenia and Croatia? There were arguments both for and against. The British diplomat Lord Carrington, who was trying to arrange an all-Yugoslav settlement, predicted what would happen:

'An early recognition of Croatia would undoubtedly mean the breakup of the conference ... There is also a real danger that Bosnia-Herzegovina would also ask for independence or recognition, which would be wholly unacceptable to the Serbs in the republic ... This might well be the spark that sets Bosnia-Herzegovina alight.'

It has often been claimed that this was a blunder. Once Slovenia and Croatia had gone, the other republics were bound to follow. And once it was clear that Yugoslavia was doomed, minorities would grow fearful, while politicians scrambled for as much power and territory as they could get during the breakup. This is certainly what happened, with disastrous results.

Croatian Jasmina Ramic remarked: 'My best friend was a Serb. Then he went to the federal army and now shoots at us. I had a lot of Serb friends before, but it can never be like that again.'

THE BOSNIAN CRISIS

Hopes and fears, 1990-1

In Bosnia, the largest ethnic groups were the Muslims (43 per cent), the Serbs (31 per cent) and the Croats (17 per cent). When elections were held in 1990, most Bosnians voted for ethnic-based political parties – the Party of Democratic Action (Muslim), the Serbian Democratic Party and the Croatian Democratic Union (which highlighted its loyalties by choosing the same name as Tudjman's party in Croatia itself). This suggested that being a member of an ethnic group had become more important than being a Bosnian or Yugoslav citizen.

Alija Izetbegovic (centre), President of Bosnia, at prayer during a Muslim service.

The three ethnic parties had worked together to defeat the Communist and pro-federal parties. They dominated the Bosnian parliament and for a time shared power. Alija Izetbegovic, a Muslim and the leader of the largest party (the Party of Democratic Action), became the president of Bosnia.

When Yugoslavia started to break up, the situation in Bosnia became tense. During the 1991 war, the Bosnian Serbs supported the Serb rebels in Croatia, whereas the Bosnian Muslims and Croats condemned them. The Bosnian Serbs wanted to stay in the Yugoslav federation. The Muslims and Croats believed that this meant submitting to Serb domination – especially if Slovenia and Croatia were allowed to break away, leaving a smaller Yugoslavia with an overwhelming Serb-Montenegrin majority.

Izetbegovic of Bosnia

Alija Izetbegovic (1925-), a Muslim lawyer, became the president of Bosnia in 1990.

On the basis of his earlier writings, he was accused by his enemies of seeking Muslim domination of Bosnia.

As president, he championed a multi-ethnic society as the only way to hold the republic together. Even at the height of the Bosnian Serbs' military successes, he was determined to fight on:

'If we capitulate, we will either be captured or be killed. We have no choice, no alternative.'

Each group in Bosnia had its own fears and hopes. The Bosnian Serbs claimed that Izetbegovic wanted to make them obey Muslim laws and customs. Izetbegovic presented himself as a moderate who believed that all religions should be treated equally. But some of his words and actions were of a kind to make Serbs suspicious. In July 1991, for example, Izetbegovic tried to make Bosnia a member of the Organization of Islamic States, as though he regarded Bosnia as part of the Muslim world. He may not have meant this, but his action helped to strengthen the Bosnian Serbs' opposition to an independent Bosnia in which they would be a minority.

March 1994: after two years in their besieged city, the people of Sarajevo still hoped for peace and were still prepared to come into the streets and show their feelings.

In spite of Serb opposition, it seemed more and more likely that Bosnia would break away from Yugoslavia. The Bosnian Serbs began to prepare for a conflict, seizing large areas and running them on their own. Even before there was any serious fighting, a Serb-run 'republic' began to come into existence.

Bosnia becomes independent

By January 1992 Slovenia and Croatia were being recognized by other countries as independent states. They had succeeded in breaking away from Yugoslavia, and this meant that the Bosnian Muslims and Croats would soon try to do the same.

Izetbegovic realized that a declaration of independence might lead to a war inside Bosnia unless he could make an agreement with the Serbs in the republic. Talks were held at Lisbon in Portugal, and in February 1992 Izetbegovic accepted a compromise arranged by the European Community. The Serbs would not try to break up Bosnia, but the country would be reorganized so that Muslims, Croats and Serbs would each occupy and control their own territories. It was not clear how this could be done peacefully, since there were so many areas of mixed population that did not obviously 'belong' to any one group. But when Izetbegovic changed his mind about the deal, the Bosnian Serbs and Croats were understandably angry, and a chance of keeping the peace may have been lost.

The Bosnian Serb leader Radovan Karadzic, 1995.

Instead, the Bosnians were asked to vote for or against a break with the Yugoslav federation. The Bosnian Serbs boycotted (refused to take part in) the vote, so there was a big majority for independence. On 3 March 1992 Bosnia was declared a sovereign republic.

Armed clashes began almost at once, but for a time the situation remained confused – neither real peace nor all-out war. Then, on 6-7 April, the European Community recognized Bosnia, ending any possibility that the republic might still remain part of Yugoslavia. Immediately the Bosnian Serb leader, Radovan Karadzic, declared that the Serb-held territories were breaking away from Bosnia to form a separate republic.

Karadzic, leader of the Bosnian Serbs

Born in Montenegro, Radovan Karadzic (1945-), poet and psychiatrist, became the leader of the main Bosnian Serb political party, the Serbian Democratic Party, in 1990.

As spokesman for the Bosnian Serbs, he always denied Serb atrocities and tried to blame them on the Muslims or Croats. There was strong evidence that many war crimes were committed on his orders, or at least with his knowledge. Behind his fanatical policy lay the belief that:

'Serbs and Muslims are like cats and dogs. They cannot live together in peace. It's impossible.'

The new Yugoslavia

Once Bosnia had left the federation, the old Yugoslavia was dead. At the end of April 1992, Serbia and Montenegro formed a new Yugoslav federation, less than half the size of the one before. The aim of the Bosnian and Croatian Serbs was now to join the new federation, bringing with them as much territory as they could hold and creating a 'Greater Serbia'.

The new Yugoslav Federation (1992-) and its neighbours.

A Serb militiaman throws a hand grenade through the window of a house.

The war begins

During April and May 1992, a Serb offensive raged in northern and eastern Bosnia. The Serbs' aim was to conquer these areas and 'cleanse' them of their Muslim and Croat inhabitants. Threats, brutalities and killings drove civilians from their homes. Most of them were women, children and old people; the young and fit men were arrested and disappeared.

The worst atrocities were again committed by militias such as the Tigers. As in Croatia, the Yugoslav army usually sided with the Serbs. Now that so many republics had broken away from Yugoslavia, the army was an overwhelmingly Serb force, but there were still some commanders who thought of themselves as Yugoslavs whose duty was to keep the peace.

A Croat refugee leaves her bombed-out home in West Mostar.

Civilians beaten and murdered

Accounts of massacres and tortures in Bosnia are almost
unbearable to read. Some of the worst treatment was inflicted on
civilians, even though such actions were against international
law. This account is by a Muslim man who survived after all the
male Muslims in his village were rounded up and herded into the
local elementary school. To begin with there were 500 or 600 of
them, and more were brought in from time to time. Serb
militiamen attacked them, raining down blows with iron bars.

'Those who had been beaten up were taken out, thrown into a
skip and burned alive. Then they placed the skip under our
window. The bodies were transported by van and lorry and then
thrown into the [river] Drina. The survivors were bound together
in tens and around 120 or 130 were slung into a lorry. The Serb
militia from Bratunak then drove us to Pale. The local Serbs in
Pale screamed, "Give us the Ustashas so we can slaughter them!"
Then for the first time they made a list of us. Altogether there
were only 430 of us left. We were taken into some gym where we
spent three days. Then they bound us again and took us in lorries
to Visoko ... There were 399 of us left when we arrived at Visoko.
They exchanged us civilians for Chetnik fighters.'

These differences of attitude within the Yugoslav army
added to the complications in an already confused
situation. In May, Bosnian Serb forces surrounded the
Bosnian capital, Sarajevo. But a Yugoslav general,
Milutin Kukanjac, was trapped, along with 400 of his
men, at a barracks in the city. Though he had tried not
to take sides in the ethnic conflict, he and his men
were in great danger. However, the airport was under
army control, and so, when President Izetbegovic
landed there after taking part in talks abroad, Kukanjac
took the desperate decision to have him arrested. The
local United Nations commander, General Lewis
Mackenzie, was called in and helped to arrange a
swap: Kukanjac and his men would be released in
exchange for the president. Both leaders and the

soldiers left the barracks in a convoy, but Bosnian government supporters either misunderstood the situation or deliberately broke the agreement. They cut off the convoy, killing a number of the Yugoslav soldiers trapped in their vehicles.

Serb victims

Most people who knew about the situation in former Yugoslavia felt that the Serbs were the worst aggressors and ethnic cleansers. Eventually it became hard to convince people in other countries that other groups could also commit atrocities. The BBC reporter Martin Bell discovered this when he rang his newsroom in London and described the killing of Yugoslav army men during the Izetbegovic-Kukanjac exchange. A voice at the other end questioned every statement he made. Finally Bell said:

'Look, this is the Balkans. Perhaps it's not as simple as you would like it to be, but Serbs can be victims too.'

The victims of the war came from all the different peoples in the war zones. Here, in 1991, Serbs are forced to leave their homes in Croatia.

By May, Kukanjac's neutral attitude was already unusual. The army was Serb-dominated and working with Milosevic, the president of Serbia, and the pro-Serb federal leadership. During the war in Croatia, and then when trouble started in Bosnia, Milosevic insisted that the actions of the army and the Serb militias had nothing to do with him. When UN negotiators asked him to stop the Bosnian Serbs attacking towns and villages, he replied that he would do what he could, but that he had no authority over them. In theory this was true, but actually the Bosnian Serbs received much help from Serbia, as well as back-up from the Yugoslav army.

Les discours sur la purification ethnique, ça ne vous rappelle rien ?

HALTE AUX CRIMES CONTRE L'HUMANITÉ DES NATIONALISTES SERBES

'Doesn't talk of ethnic cleansing remind you of anything?' asked a poster in December 1992. (Left: Hitler. Right: Milosevic.)

Rumour and propaganda

During the wars, rumour and propaganda played on people's fears. A Reuters newsman, Andrej Gustincic, was shown a field by a Serbian woman in Foca. She told him:

'The jihad [Muslim Holy War] was supposed to begin there. Foca was going to be the new Mecca. There were lists of Serbs who were marked for death ... My two sons were down on the list to be slaughtered like pigs. I was listed under rape.'

All the Serbs in the town believed that these lists existed – but none had ever seen them. Where had such ideas come from? The historian Noel Malcolm (in his book *A Short History of Bosnia*) suggested that television had played its part:

'Having travelled widely in Bosnia over 15 years, I cannot believe the claim that the country was forever seething with ethnic hatreds. But having watched Radio Television Belgrade in the period 1991-2, I can understand why simple Bosnian Serbs came to believe that they were under threat, from Ustasha hordes, fundamentalist jihads or whatever.'

The Serbs' success

In May 1992, pressure from other countries forced the Yugoslav army to withdraw from Bosnia. But the Serbs had laid their plans carefully. They had made sure that most of the army recruits in Bosnia were Bosnian-born Serbs. Bosnia was no longer part of Yugoslavia. So when the army withdrew, these men could be left behind in their native land – along with their equipment and weaponry. They formed an 80,000-strong force of trained fighters that gave the Bosnian Serbs an enormous advantage over their enemies.

In most places the Serbs seemed unstoppable. By the end of August, 60-70 per cent of Bosnia was in Serb hands and was rapidly being emptied of Muslims and Croats. The Serbs had also achieved one of their most important objectives – to establish a corridor linking Serb-held territory in Croatia and northern Bosnia with Serb lands further east. As isolated 'islands' of Serb territory, surrounded by enemies, they could not survive in the long run. Linked up with other areas, they would form part of a single 'Greater Serbia'.

Sarajevans fight to buy bread after a cease-fire in May 1992.

By the time the harsh Bosnian winter set in, the Serbs had achieved most of their aims. But the Muslims had held on to a strip of land in the east which included Srebrenica, Gorazde and other towns crowded with refugees. And Sarajevo, though surrounded and bombarded, was still in Bosnian government hands.

TERROR AND TRAGEDY

Croats against Muslims

During 1992 the Serbs had been fighting both the Muslims and the Croats in Bosnia. There were large numbers of Bosnian Croats in the west of the republic, especially around the city of Mostar, and here the Serbs had been heavily defeated and driven back. But Croats and Muslims did not work together for long. In October 1992 the Croats began to attack Muslim areas. Like the Serbs, they received help from across the border – in this case, from the Croatian republic. The Muslims, under attack from two sides, soon controlled only a tenth of Bosnia.

Fighting resumes, 1993

After a winter lull, fighting became intense again in the spring of 1993. The Serbs continued to hammer at Sarajevo, but they made more progress in attacking the territory around Srebrenica in eastern Bosnia. This was one of the isolated areas, deep in Serb-controlled territory, where Muslim refugees had gathered.

Sarajevo: UN soldiers try to ensure that people can cross the road, safe from sniper fire.

By mid-April Srebrenica could hold out no longer. The city surrendered and its defenders handed over their arms. But there was no massacre, and the Muslims were not driven out. This was because the United Nations (UN) had acted at last. On 16 April 1993 the UN declared Srebrenica a 'safe area' whose inhabitants could not be attacked or made to leave. Later, the UN named more safe areas: Sarajevo, Tuzla, Bihac, Zepa and Gorazde. In reality, there were not enough UN troops to resist a Serb attack on Srebrenica, and the city remained surrounded and helpless. For the moment the Serbs were not willing to risk the world's anger by attacking Srebrenica, but they might well do so later, at a more favourable time.

The UN's role in Yugoslavia

People almost everywhere in the world had been outraged by ethnic cleansing and other horrors taking place in Yugoslavia. They hoped that the United Nations, which represents all the countries and peoples of the world, would put a stop to these terrible things. When this did not happen, they blamed the UN for failing to take proper action. But its position was more difficult than it seemed. The UN has little power of its own. Its troops, equipment and money are supplied by its member nations – and those nations are not always generous. They also prefer not to risk the lives of their soldiers, unless their own interests are involved. Therefore the UN is often short of soldiers even for peace-keeping tasks.

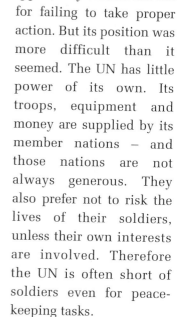

This scarecrow has been put up to warn people to keep away from a no-man's-land between Serb and Croat forces near Karlovac.

In practice, the UN has two main roles. One is to try to end conflicts by arranging truces and talks and putting forward peace plans. The other is to send in a peacekeeping force to separate the warring sides or protect helpless people such as the civilians trapped in Sarajevo.

UN peacekeepers are normally sent in only if both sides in a conflict will accept them. In Yugoslavia they had to avoid taking sides, and were expected not to use their weapons – sometimes not even in self-defence.

These UN lorries are taking Muslim refugees from Srebrenica to Tuzla. The boy running along has fallen from one of them.

This meant that peacekeepers and protectors had little real power to enforce a truce, to hold back an attack, or to stop militiamen mistreating civilians. UN peace-keeping was dependent on the co-operation of the people who were fighting, and in Croatia and Bosnia many of them were not ready for peace. The best that the UN could do was to rescue civilians by organizing convoys to take them to a safer place. This was often done, although it actually helped the militias get rid of ethnic groups in villages and towns that they wanted to 'cleanse'. In order to save lives, the UN found itself doing the 'cleansing'.

Not-so-safe areas

Critics of the UN were not impressed when Srebrenica and other places were declared 'safe areas'. Instead of stopping Serb aggression, the UN was just providing refuges for the victims – and refuges that the UN did not send in enough troops to protect. The Venezuelan ambassador to the UN, Diego Arria, said:

'We should call them what they are: ghettos, refugee camps, open jails, areas under threat; but we should never be so brazen as to call them "safe areas".'

Defending the United Nations

The UN was strongly criticized for the way it acted in former Yugoslavia. But a British commander who served with the UN, Lieutenant-Colonel Bob Stewart, pointed out that the UN mainly deals with problems that nobody seems able to solve:

'Everyone expects so much of the United Nations, especially when it comes to solving the problems of the world. This was particularly so in Bosnia. The truth is that it is only because problems are so intractable [stubborn] that we look to the United Nations for a resolution. If there were straightforward solutions to such breakdowns in human affairs, they would have been cleared up long before.'

The only alternative would have been for the UN itself to take military action – to send in troops to fight on one side or the other or to force all the warring parties to lay down their arms. None of the great powers wanted this kind of dangerous involvement. Air attacks were a more realistic possibility, for example launched against the Serbs who besieged 'safe areas'. But even these were rejected for a long time because they might be answered by attacks on the peacekeepers working on the ground in Bosnia.

French UN soldiers in Croatia, searching for booby traps and mines.

As it became clear that millions of people were suffering because of the war in Bosnia, the UN decision not to intervene in force was widely criticized. So was the decision to ban sales of arms to former Yugoslavia. In Bosnia the Serbs were already heavily armed, so the ban made it harder for the Bosnian government forces to resist. This was unjust, yet it was also true that the more weapons there were in the area, the more lives would be lost.

One aim of UN policy was to stop Serbia interfering in the Bosnian war. In May 1992 UN sanctions (measures intended to punish) were put into place against Serbia and Montenegro. Countries were told not to trade with them, and in particular not to supply them with oil. As a result, the Yugoslav army was supposedly withdrawn from Bosnia (see page 38), but this did not satisfy the UN and sanctions remained in force, hurting the Serbian economy. At this stage in the conflict, it was widely believed that Milosevic was directing the entire Serb effort in the Croatian and Bosnian wars. If so, punishing Serbia might make him change his policy. His ambitions certainly did a great deal to destroy the old Yugoslavia and stir up ethnic hatreds, but later events showed that Serbs in Croatia and Bosnia would not tamely follow his orders.

British UN soldiers remove bodies from a burned-out home in a village near Vitez in Bosnia.

From 1992 onwards, UN troops were deeply involved in former Yugoslavia. 14,000 peacekeepers were sent to Croatia to make sure that the war did not start again. Members of UNPROFOR (UN Protection Force) were stationed in Sarajevo, where the Bosnian Serbs handed over the airport, enabling food and medical supplies to be brought in for the besieged citizens. Other UN troops escorted convoys carrying supplies to populations that were close to starvation. It was dangerous work which involved getting through many checkpoints and roadblocks manned by trigger-happy militiamen, and some UN soldiers were in fact killed.

A journalist amid a group of Croat fighters.

66   Reporting from the front line

The wars in former Yugoslavia involved much sniping and street fighting. News reporters often came under fire, and dozens were killed or injured. In an interview with Anne Seba, BBC TV reporter Kate Adie described one of her experiences:

'... that autumn [1991] I didn't think I would get through the night. There were mortars, rockets and shells every second and I found myself unable to breathe properly. In the end I curled up ... and then buried my head under a blanket in the dark with the fleas and mosquitoes.'

In Sarajevo, BBC TV reporter Martin Bell was wounded by mortar fire:

'I had always wondered what it would be like to be wounded and now I knew ... It was like an acute pain in the abdomen, though somewhat numbed by the shock of it. I had been struck by two or three fragments of shrapnel ... I was knocked to the ground by the force of the impact ... Don [the cameraman] continued the shooting of what would be my last news story for a while.'

99

Camera, lights, action

Modern wars are reported by the media – newspapers, radio and, above all, television, which can show vivid scenes of battle and death. When people in foreign countries see these things, they are often angered or horrified. If they feel strongly enough, their governments may take notice. So the fighters may start to behave in a way that will influence foreign television audiences.

BBC reporter Martin Bell thought that this happened many times in former Yugoslavia. A Croat general launched an attack when reporters were present. Bell has written:

'The Croats were campaigning for international recognition, and it suited their purpose to be seen fighting off marauding Serbs ... Did the battle occur just while we were there, or because we were there?'

News coverage of the war

Thanks to newspapers and television, people knew about the misery in Bosnia and wanted to help. Individuals as well as official agencies brought in food, clothing and other necessities. But news coverage also told the world about the terrible things being done – things that particularly upset Europeans, who liked to think that their continent was a special, civilized place.

As well as humanitarian agencies, individuals did their best to help the suffering Bosnians. One such individual was a British woman, Sally Becker, seen here with a child from Mostar in western Bosnia. During bitter fighting between Croats and Muslims, Becker took considerable personal risks to rescue groups of children, most of them in urgent need of medical attention.

The evil of 'ethnic cleansing'

Ethnic cleansing – uprooting entire populations – was known about from an early date. In Bosnia, the main 'cleansers' were Bosnian Serb militiamen, and the main victims were Muslims and Croats. But inevitably, once it had started, Muslims and Croats often acted just as brutally in places where they were strong.

Serbs and Croats tried to destroy each other's way of life. Serbs destroyed this Catholic church in Croatia.

Sudden killings or wholesale massacres, arrests and tortures drove villagers from their homes. If people of different ethnic groups seemed to be living peacefully together, militiamen came in from outside and did the 'cleansing'. During these operations, Serb militiamen often forced Serb villagers to take part in killings, destroying the trust that had existed between neighbours. In the larger towns, it was harder to assemble and drive out the entire population. Instead, people were encouraged to leave by fear-creating campaigns, ranging from petty humiliations to blowing up their houses. Before they were allowed to go, they often had to sign documents giving up their rights to their property. Bulldozers levelled village houses, and mosques and churches were blown up. The intention was that, whatever happened, those who left would have no reason ever to come back to their old homes.

The camps exposed

One of those who visited the Serb-run detention camp at Omarska was a British journalist, Ed Vulliamy. The guards had obviously tried to make the camp look a reasonable place, and the prisoners were too frightened to talk about what had been done to them. But Vulliamy was still horrified by what he saw.

'The men are at various stages of human decay ... the bones of their elbows and wrists protrude like pieces of jagged stone from the pencil thin stalks to which their arms have been reduced ... There is nothing quite like the sight of the prisoner desperate to talk and to convey some terrible truth ... but who dares not. Their stares burn, they speak only with their terrified silence ...'

In July and August 1992 an American journalist claimed that many thousands of Muslims were being held at camps where the treatment and conditions were like those of Nazi extermination camps. Described by the Serbs as prisoners of war, the Muslims were mostly male villagers rounded up during ethnic cleansing.

Muslim prisoners at Manjaca camp.

At the camps, senseless killings and beatings were common. But more systematic crimes were also committed. The most important people in the former Muslim communities, including those who were wealthy or educated, were picked out and killed. The plan was obviously to leave the Muslim community leaderless for years to come. Other prisoners, if they survived long enough, could hope to be exchanged for Serb prisoners of war.

This man was lucky: he survived a Serb camp where the prisoners were starved. Eventually he was transferred to a camp where inmates were at least provided with food and medical supplies. Here, finally released, he is reunited with his family.

The Bosnian Serb leader, Radovan Karadzic, denied that conditions in the camps were bad, and invited reporters and cameramen to go to see for themselves. Even though the Serbs tried to show the camps at their best, pictures of men like skeletons shocked the world and hardened feelings against the Serbs. Then evidence of new atrocities appeared – the rape of Muslim women in a Bosnian Serb camp. Rape is violent sexual assault. Individual examples, usually against women, occur in most wars. But in Bosnia it was not an individual crime: like the killings in the camps, it was a deliberate policy. And the evidence suggested that members of the Bosnian Serb leadership were deeply involved.

Drugs and drink

Many fighters in Croatia and Bosnia were 'high' on drugs and drink. Their effects may have made it easier to carry out inhuman actions. According to a Macedonian officer in the Yugoslav army (see page 26):

'If ever we took a Croat position, there was always evidence of drug taking.'

An outside observer, Robert Fox, testified that:

'In two years in Bosnia and Croatia I have rarely come across a group of soldiery, Serb, Croat or Muslim, who have been entirely sober.'

Murder, torture and rape are war crimes, punishable under international law. Many people now believed that trials should be held of Bosnian Serbs and any other soldiers or politicians who were war criminals. But while the war raged, the UN was more concerned to try to stop it. Two plans were proposed in 1993. One would have kept Bosnia together, dividing the country into ten mostly self-governing areas. The Serbs rejected it. The other plan, put forward by Milosevic and Tudjman, would have broken up Bosnia into three states, organized along ethnic lines. Although hard-pressed, Izetbegovic's government finally rejected the idea. The war went on.

Rape

Many rapes were carried out on women at the Foca camp. One Muslim woman described her experience. Still recovering from a shrapnel wound, she was taken to a room by a local factory worker.

'He ripped open my shirt and started prodding the wound on my chest with the butt of his gun, saying "Now I'm going to rape you and if you start screaming I'll kill you."'

Many rapes at Foca were followed by the murder of the victim, or of relatives who had been forced to watch.

THE QUEST FOR PEACE IN BOSNIA

A Muslim-Croat federation

The first hopeful signs appeared early in 1994. They were partly a result of the tougher attitude taken by the USA, the world's most powerful nation and the leader of the NATO military alliance. NATO was working closely with the United Nations.

American pressure on Croatia helped to bring about an agreement between the Bosnian Croats and Izetbegovic's government. Consequently, on 1 March 1994, the two agreed to form a Muslim-Croat federation. It was not clear how well the federation would work, but at least the Muslims had one enemy the less and could smuggle in weapons for their troops through Croatia.

This man makes artificial limbs. During the four-year-long siege of Sarajevo he was busier than he had ever been before.

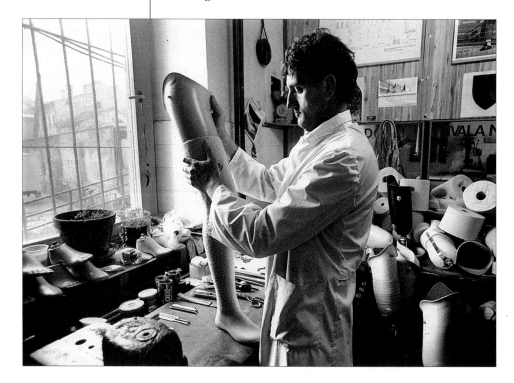

Life under siege

Sarajevo was besieged by the Bosnian Serbs for almost four years. The British journalist Christopher Hitchens summed up life in the city:

'The daily round in Sarajevo is one of dodging snipers, scrounging food and water, collecting rumours, visiting morgues and blood banks and joking heavily about near misses.'

Sarajevo, 1994: taking a dangerous trip to collect water. The buildings are peppered with bullet and shrapnel holes.

NATO becomes involved

While the Muslims and Croats were making peace, the Bosnian Serbs came under pressure to end the siege of Sarajevo. On 5 February a Serb mortar bomb fell on a market place in the city centre. It proved unusually deadly, killing 69 people and injuring more than 200. About 10,000 people had already died in Sarajevo, but this one sensational incident, reported on television all over the world, made people very angry. Their leaders felt that they now had to act, and NATO issued threats that eventually persuaded the Serbs to stop bombarding the city and pull back their heavy weapons out of range of Sarajevo.

Over the next few months there were many clashes between the Bosnian Serbs and NATO and the UN. A number of air strikes were launched against the Serbs, who bluffed, made promises, dragged out negotiations, and on one occasion even took UN soldiers as hostages. Their delaying tactics seemed to work, and they continued to make gains, notably around the 'safe area' of Gorazde. Most of this Muslim stronghold fell to the fanatical Serb commander, General Mladic, but the threat of action by NATO did stop him from occupying the city itself.

September 1995: a cruise missile being launched against the Serb stronghold of Banja Luka from the USS *Normandy,* an American warship in the Adriatic.

The Bosnian Serbs suffered an important setback when Milosevic of Serbia withdrew his support. In July 1994 the great powers proposed a division of Bosnia that would have given the Serbs 49 per cent of the republic and the Muslim-Croat federation 51 per cent. Milosevic wanted the Bosnian Serbs to agree, but they would not give up any of the territory they had won. With UN sanctions hurting Serbia badly, Milosevic was angry to find that Karadzic and his followers would not do as they were told, and that the chance of a favourable settlement was being lost. Hoping that sanctions would be lifted, he stopped helping the Bosnian Serbs and even cut off trade links with them.

The war turns against the Serbs

The war in Bosnia dragged on until December 1994, when Jimmy Carter, a former US president, managed to arrange a cease-fire. For the next four months there was some fighting, but no all-out struggle. Unexpectedly, this proved to be a turning-point in the conflict.

In May, the war in Croatia flared up again. A re-equipped Croat army launched an offensive against the Serb-occupied areas of the country. During their summer campaign the Croats overwhelmed the Serbs and eventually recovered all the territory they had lost. Now it was the Serbs who became the victims of atrocities condemned by the UN. And in a huge ethnic cleansing, at least 150,000 Croatian Serbs fled from their homes and took refuge in Bosnia and Serbia.

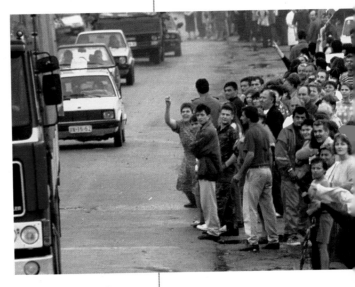

August 1995: a crowd of Croats jeer at Serb refugees as they pass through Sisak in Bosnia, on their way to Serbia.

The war also began to go badly for the Serbs in Bosnia. In spite of this, in July they defied the UN by overrunning the safe area of Srebrenica, massacring thousands of Muslim men. As so often, they went unpunished because NATO was paralysed by differences of opinion between the great powers. Then, on 28 August, a shell landed in another Sarajevo market, killing 38 people. Again the smaller tragedy

The crime of Srebrenica

Thousands of Muslim men were executed after the fall of Srebrenica. Charging the Bosnian Serb leaders with 'one of the bloodiest acts in the war', Christian Chartier, the spokesman for the War Crimes Tribunal (see page 56) declared:

'These crimes were committed by the Bosnian Serb forces under the control of Radovan Karadzic. He authorized the attack and the subsequent criminal actions. These crimes were carried out by the Bosnian Serb forces under the command of Ratko Mladic who was seen at several locations ... where systematic mass killings took place.'

made more of an impact, and NATO replied with a series of heavy bombing raids on Bosnian Serb positions, mainly those surrounding – and menacing – the safe areas.

The presidents of Serbia, Bosnia and Croatia sign the Dayton peace agreement on 21 November 1995.

The Dayton peace agreement

By now even the Bosnian Serbs had had enough. They agreed to work with Milosevic again, this time in serious peace talks. In fact, the main negotiations took place between the Serb, Croat and Bosnian governments, without any direct part being played by the Bosnian Serbs or Bosnian Croats. The talks, held in the USA, were influenced by strong American pressure on all the parties involved. By October there was a complete cease-fire, and on 21 November 1995, at Dayton, Ohio, Izetbegovic, Milosevic and Tudjman signed an agreement intended to bring peace and settle Bosnia's future.

FUTURE UNCERTAIN

The agreement at Dayton laid down that Bosnia was to remain a single state. But it was to consist of two parts, the Muslim-Croat federation (51 per cent of Bosnia) and the Serb 'republic' (49 per cent). Each of the main ethnic groups would have a representative on a three-person presidency. Elections would be held as soon as possible. Human rights would be respected, including the right of refugees to return to their homes or be compensated for their losses. Peace would be ensured by the presence in Bosnia of a 60,000-strong NATO force.

The agreement was carried out fairly smoothly. But the handing over of all of Sarajevo to Muslim control enraged Sarajevan Serbs. Thousands left, and Serbs who did stay found themselves bullied by Muslim gangs. In most parts of Bosnia, ethnic cleansing had already done its work, separating the different peoples of the republic. Events in Sarajevo suggested that it would be very difficult for them ever to live side by side again.

March 1996: a Serb family flees Sarajevo.

" Serbs flee Sarajevo

Were the Serbs being over-fearful when they fled from Sarajevo in February and March 1996? Some outsiders believed they would be fools to stay. The commander of the United Nations forces in the city was a French soldier, Jean-René Bachelet. Three months earlier he had warned bluntly that:

'For many Serbs the only choice will be between the suitcase and the coffin.' **"**

War criminals

While elections were being arranged, an international court, set up by the United Nations in 1993, began to hold trials for war crimes. Among those charged were the Bosnian Serb leader, Radovan Karadzic, and the military commander, General Ratko Mladic. But neither of them was arrested. The NATO troops could hold wanted men if they came into their hands, but they were not supposed to go looking for war criminals. Though nobody admitted it, there were political reasons for this state of affairs. Arresting Karadzic – especially before elections were held – might have angered the Serbs and endangered the entire peace process. Karadzic continued to live at his headquarters, Pale, close to Sarajevo. He was forced to give up his leadership of the Serbian Democratic Party, but it was said that he still had great influence behind the scenes.

During his trial by the UN International Tribunal at The Hague, Bosnian Serb Dusan Tadic sits inside a bullet-proof glass enclosure. He was charged with crimes against Muslim civilians at Omarska and other camps in north-west Bosnia.

Elections

Elections were held throughout Bosnia in September 1996. Many outside observers thought that this was too soon. Parties based on non-ethnic ideas such as liberalism and social democracy made little progress while memories of atrocities were still fresh. The elections ended in victory for the same ethnic-based parties that had triumphed in 1990 – and the leaders of the Bosnian Serbs and Croats hardly bothered to hide their aim of breaking up the Bosnian state. In the presidential election, Alija Izetbegovic won the most votes and therefore became the chairman of the three-person presidency.

Going back home

When Muslims chose to vote in the places where they had once lived, they were rarely allowed even a glimpse of their old homes. At Doboj, Mehmed Cajic said:

'It feels like I have just come on to foreign soil, like a visitor. It is a painful feeling.'

Others were defiant. Saban, returning to Visegrad, said:

'I want to see my home for the first time in more than four years. I'm going back to vote there to show that I want to live there again. It can be in peace or we will fight for it again.'

Politically not much seemed to have changed in six years. But the landscape was very different, filled with ruined towns and burned-out, bulldozed villages. And although there were fewer areas of mixed population than in 1990, Bosnia was a land where large numbers of refugees still hoped to go home. During the elections, the Bosnian Serb leadership encouraged Serb refugees to vote in the area to which they had fled, so that the Serb grip on such areas would be strengthened. But some Muslims insisted on voting in the places where they had lived before being driven out. Guarded by NATO troops, they travelled back and managed to cast their votes. Their unfriendly reception in such places made it hard to see how they could ever return in safety, even though this had been agreed at Dayton.

After the elections

After the 1996 elections, Joe Wilson, a British member of the European Parliament, said bluntly:

'Bosnia has died, rebirth is impossible. The future will be a greater Serbia, a greater Croatia and a smaller but deeper problem in the middle.'

However, most NATO leaders preferred to see the holding of elections as a victory for democracy. Early in October 1996, sanctions against Yugoslavia (Serbia and Montenegro) were lifted, and Yugoslavia and Bosnia recognized each other and established normal relations.

The future still seemed impossible to predict. At the end of 1996 there were a million refugees in Bosnia and many more in other countries. While NATO forces remained in Bosnia – and they seemed likely to stay there for a long time – the political situation might well be stable. And, in the long run, rebuilding their devastated country might bring Bosnia's peoples together. These were hopes, not certainties. The only certainty was that a hard road lay ahead.

Facing the future

At the end of the war, President Izetbegovic remained convinced that Bosnia's peoples could still live side by side again.

'We do not see this as difficult. We are used to living like this. We were attending classes together with people who had different names, a different religion or nationality. None of this is strange to us.'

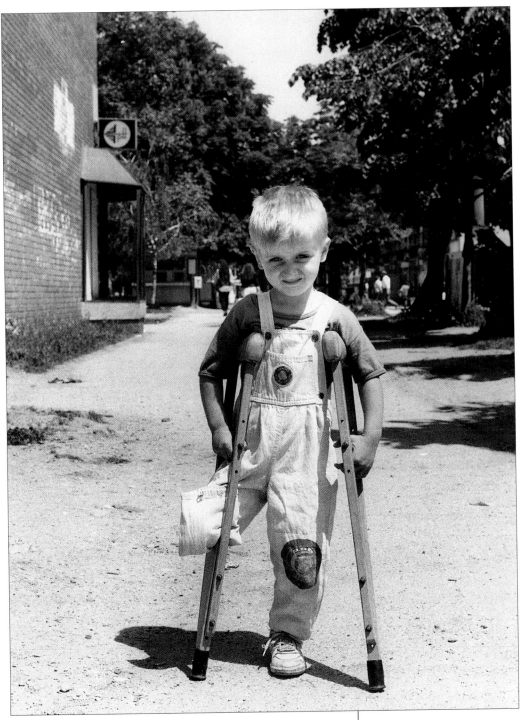

Aladin, one of more than two thousand children left disabled by the war in Bosnia.

DATE LIST

1990

January — League of Communists, near collapse, allows free elections.

April — Nationalists win elections in Slovenia.

May — Nationalist CDU victorious in Croatian elections; Tudjman becomes president.

November — Milosevic and allies win elections in Serbia and Montenegro.
Nationalist parties triumph in Bosnia and Macedonia.

December — Slovenians vote in favour of independence.

1991

May — Croatian referendum in favour of independence.

June — Croatia and Slovenia declare independence. Croatian Serbs vote to break away from Croatia; fighting in the republic becomes intense.
Yugoslav army fails in bid to take over Slovenia.

September — Macedonia declares independence.

October — Bosnian parliament votes in favour of independence.

November — UN takes over peacekeeping efforts in Yugoslavia from EC.

December — Germany declares it will recognize Slovenia and Croatia.

1992

January — EC recognizes Slovenia and Croatia.

March — Bosnians vote for independence; boycotted by Bosnian Serbs.

April — Fighting in Bosnia between Serbs and others; siege of Sarajevo begins. USA and EC recognize Bosnia. Serbia and Montenegro form new federal Yugoslavia.

May — UN sanctions against Yugoslavia.

July — UN takes over Sarajevo airport to bring in supplies.

August — First reports of atrocities in Bosnian Serb prison camps.

September — Yugoslavia suspended from UN.

October — Bosnian Croats, supported by Croat government, begin attacks on Muslim positions.

December — Milosevic re-elected president of Serbia.

1993

January — Vance-Owen peace plan for 'federal' Bosnia.

April — Collapse of Muslim resistance around Srebrenica. UN declares Srebrenica a 'safe area'.

June — Following failure of Vance-Owen plan, Milosevic and Tudjman put forward partition plan.
Fierce Croat-Muslim fighting, especially around Mostar.

September — Milosevic-Tudjman plan rejected.

1994	
February	Under NATO pressure Bosnian Serbs agree to withdraw from Sarajevo; their failure to do so fully causes many clashes in following months. Muslim-Croat cease-fire.
March	Muslim-Croat federation formed.
April	NATO bombs Serb forces attacking Goradze.
July	Bosnian Serbs reject international peace plan backed by Milosevic.
September	Bosnian Serb pressure on Sarajevo leads to NATO air strikes, met by Serb attacks on peacekeepers.
December	Cease-fire in Bosnia, arranged by Jimmy Carter.
1995	
May	End of cease-fires in Bosnia and Croatia.

1995	NATO bombs Bosnian Serb ammunition dumps; Bosnian Serbs take UN peacekeepers as hostages.
May *cont.*	
July	Bosnian Serbs overrun Srebrenica; mass killings reported.
August	Croat offensive crushes opposition in eastern Croatia; Serbs in flight. Serb shelling of Sarajevo leads to NATO bombing raids. Bosnian Serbs agree to negotiate for peace.
October	Cease-fire in Croatia and Bosnia.
December	Dayton peace agreement.
1996	
May	First trial for war crimes begins at The Hague.
September	Elections held throughout Bosnia.

SOURCES

The following were used as sources of information for this book:

Rabia Ali and Lawrence Lifschultz (eds.), *Why Bosnia? Writings on the Balkan War*, The Pamphleteer's Press, Conn., 1993
Mark Almond, *Europe's Backyard War: the war in the Balkans*, Heinemann, 1994
Martin Bell, *In Harm's Way: reflections of a war zone thug*, Hamish Hamilton, 1995
Mischa Glenny, *The Fall of Yugoslavia: the third Balkan War*, Penguin, rev.ed., 1993
Roy Gutman, *A Witness to Genocide*, Element Books, 1993
Lewis Mackenzie, *Peacekeeper*, McIntyre, 1993
Branka Magas, *The Destruction of Yugoslavia: tracing the break-up 1980-92*, Verso, 1993

Noel Malcolm, *Bosnia: A Short History*, Macmillan, rev.ed., 1996
Edgar O'Ballance, *Civil War in Bosnia*, St Martin's Press, 1995
David Rieff, *Slaughterhouse: Bosnia and the failure of the West*, Vintage, 1995
Laura Silber and Allan Little, *The Death of Yugoslavia*, Penguin Books/BBC Books, 1995
Lt-Col. Bob Stewart, *Broken Lives: a personal view of the Bosnian conflict*, Harper Collins, 1993
Mark Thompson, *A Paper House: the ending of Yugoslavia*, Hutchinson/Radius, 1992; Vintage paperback, 1992.
Ed Vulliamy, *Seasons in Hell*, Simon and Schuster, 1994
Richard West, *Tito and the Rise and Fall of Yugoslavia*, Sinclair-Stevenson, 1994

GLOSSARY

Balkans all of south-east Europe to the south of Hungary and Romania.

Chetniks Yugoslav resistance fighters against the German occupation during the Second World War.
During the wars in Yugoslavia in 1991-5, some Serb militias called themselves Chetniks.

ethnic cleansing driving peoples or groups from an area so that it becomes the exclusive property of only one group. It was originally a propaganda term, intended to excuse persecution; it implied that the people driven out had somehow been polluting their 'purer' persecutors.

federation state consisting of a number of republics or provinces, each with its own government. The power of the central, or federal, government is limited.

genocide the destruction of an entire people, nation or race.

great powers the states whose size, wealth or military strength gives them the greatest influence in international affairs.

Kosovo battle in 1389, famous in Serbian history. Now a province of Serbia mainly inhabited by Albanians.

North Atlantic Treaty Organization (NATO) military alliance whose members include the USA, Canada and most west European states. Originally directed against the Soviet Union (now dissolved), it stayed in existence and played an important role in the war in Yugoslavia.

Partisans Yugoslav resistance fighters against the German occupation during the Second World War. Mainly Communists, the Partisans were rivals of the Chetniks.

Reuters famous news agency which collects and distributes news all over the world.

sanctions non-military measures taken by the international community to punish or weaken a state, usually intended to make it change its policies. Sanctions often involve a refusal to trade with the state in question.

United Nations (UN) organization that represents, and tries to bring together, all the nations of the world. It is widely involved in attempts to maintain or make peace.

INDEX